Conversations With The Mirror

Kabrina Dickey

BookLeaf
Publishing

India | USA | UK

Made with ❤ on the BookLeaf Publishing Platform

www.bookleafpub.in

www.bookleafpub.com

Dedication

To my K's.

Preface

Intimate perspective of impactful moments while processing various emotions, acknowledging undeniable truths, and conquering endless fears.

Acknowledgements

Thank you to all who have supported and believed in me.
Enjoy my Odyssey.

Amazing

I met grace before I was three,
In the song my soul, she weaved.
Angelic notes, soothing dreams,
Even now it sometimes seems,
Like you're here with me.

Options

Train your brain,
Elite mental focus.
But if you give in,
A new world unfolded,
Endless creativity,
Beyond the surface.

Running

I have this problem with over thinking,
It brings me agony,
Endlessly,
Trying to figure out what it means.
Being the missing puzzle of the masterpiece,
Never slowing down enough to see,
That life is happening concurrently.
Coincidentally,
In the end - I'll see
How it all happened,
Retroactively.

Chaos

Chaos in my brain,
Unable to attain,
The creativity I control.
Unable to abstain,
From the agony and pain,
Among the veils I patrol.

Challenge

It's time to awaken,
Step back into reality.
Escape chains of society,
Preaching how I should be.
Unable to see, the life you seek,
Into my heart, hate bleeds.
Confusion of my inhibitions,
Why am I wrong and you're the victim?
When you lack the ambition,
The grit, determination.
Preaching your own insecurities,
Lashing fear back at me.
Trying to control my fate,
Because you can't relate.

Permission

Are you mad I didn't ask for permission?
Chase the dream, all of a sudden you're missing
The forest you like to hike through,
When everything gets to you.
Pass the ferns, cedars, and pine
Come across a lake void of time.
Reflecting the moons of worlds past
The knowledge is endless, opportunity vast.
Time suspended indefinitely,
I lead you here to share my seed.
I bare my soul against the thoughts of greed,
Convince myself that I'm the key,
To unlock your every need.
Never have to face your own demons,
Bring them here, my forest will feed them.
Under the guise of release - you leave
Your problem here to grow with me.

In the dark, they transform into be,
Hate, envy, and hostility.
My safe place, my home, my salvation,
Is overrun by blind ambition.
To end this loneliness that overtakes,
I realize now, my mistake.
The demons may overturn my garden,
But it's still my fortress they choose to defend.
The darkness is something you want to forget,
To me, it's something you have to accept.
Everything deserves to be nurtured,
In the end, it'll change the future.

Fury

Blue eyes, reflecting purpose,
Challenge sparked, it isn't worth it.
Venom spewed, drenched the surface,
Powder keg, I thought you knew this.
Internal flame, undisputed,
Stoke the flame, you confuse this.
Takes the bait, Forgets purpose,
I see the game, I know the circus.
Shifting blame to pull the focus,
Let us know where the herd is.

This image of fragility that leaves you so disheartened,
Is the face of divinity to grant us all our pardons.
He'll let you speak, apologize and even make the
promise.
In the end, you know your fate, we all know where your
heart is.

Fine

When I say I'm fine, that's the truth,
That's the only version safe with you.
I never know how much to say,
Before your face goes opaque.
Jumping at the low vibration before you,
Without hearing what I'm going through.
I see you are only looking for a reason,
To defend these thoughts of treason.
Instead of wiping tears of sorrow,
It's your strength I need to borrow,
I will conquer my own battles,
You'd be surprised what I can handle.

Undecided

All the noise is getting to me,
Pointless anger, endless toxicity.
Skin porous, devil seeps into me,
Through the storm; war raged internally.
Ignored the signs;
"What is happening to me?"
Follow the light, fall into obscurity.
Try to fit in, but you're a minority,
Look around - nobody looks like me.

Box, confining.
Perspective, blinding.
Open your eyes, embrace the timing,
The wounds your unwinding,
You'll seek what you are finding.
The Truth - is the mission you're guiding,
While deciding, what I'm hiding,
The Truth is God, Hope, Faith.
It's undecided.

Grace

When you're different - you're a threat,
Grace comes in to protect.
Her hymn stirs up emotion,
Expressed as tears, complete devotion.
The one to lead you to salvation,
Grace is the one to believe in.

A little patience and creativity,
Forms a world where I can be,
Vulnerable and connect with the,
Higher power inside of me.
Weave it into a sanctuary,
Beautiful, all encompassing.
Protection from distorted energy,
As grief overtakes me,
A reunion of happiness
For a moment I forget,
I haven't lost you yet.

Grief

Frozen in a sea of indecision,
Unable to see the path, fractured vision.
A jail of agony - no provisions,
Portrays the fantasy I'm reliving.
Unfulfilled destiny, my misgivings,
Forsaken memories, me believing.
We'd always be family - dead or living,
The grief will come and go, but if you feel it,
You can share the memory and embrace it.
Don't hide away - ashamed of pain,
Unable to answer the question again.
Or face it as I fall to my knees, then
Feel the life you breathed in.
Despite hurting and hiding from the indecision,
I can see now, with perfect vision.
Grief is a state of being,
With many emotions - gamut of feelings.
You can laugh, cry and feel guilty simultaneously,
Living your life is single handedly,
The best thing you can do with grief.

Perspective

Product of circumstance,
This doesn't define you.
Chaos and happenstance,
No longer confines you.
The journey challenges,
Terrain rough.
Struggles avalanches,
"Will I ever be Enough?"
Path is winding,
Scenery closing in.
Options are blinding,
Hear an answer within;
The view I'm finding,
And taking in,
Is just a perspective,
Of the reality I'm in.

Believe

Who is God, on this land we are serving?
Looking around all I see is a disservice.
I see a cycle of endless churning,
Under the guise of learning.
We are given more than we need,
But never enough to succeed.
A constant underlying assault of doubt,
Reminding us of all we go without.
Comparisons made indefinitely,
Between the planes of society.
Fueling the tension that keeps us in motion,
We find faith and devotion.
Calming the storm that starts within.

Finally, they welcome me,
And teach me all I can be.
My purpose, my grace, my following,
A reprieve, a break, a new beginning
A system, a cycle it's never ending.
Soon, I can be enough, I can be enlightened
As long as it's verified with what they align with.
Your salvation will lead you to Heaven,
If you follow the rules, it will happen.

Happiness

How much knowledge do you really have?
Information recited on behalf.
Or maybe I might think to ask,
The powers of circumstance -
Is just a song and dance,
Distracting us from happiness.

You will have to face the truth,
The facts you quote are outside opinions spat at you.
Filling the World with the toxicity needed to fuel,
The distraction from the truth.

Shed the layer of contempt,
You make your own happiness.

Peace

Like lightning, fear strikes through me,
A bolt of electricity surging violently.
Just the slightest hint of disappointment and my world is
ablaze,
Frozen in silence while the flames rage.
An explosive amount of energy radiating from my skin,
Every ounce of emotion fueling the mindset I'm in.

Agony kills me with anticipation,
Daggers twisting while I'm waiting.
Moments passing like an eclipse,
Every sound makes me flinch.

When you're home the anxiety fades, loneliness dies,
The touch of your hand brings me to life.
The shadows will take what I can no longer fight,
Out of the darkness and into the light.
Because in your arms everything is alright.

Dreams

Endless years of conserving,
Waiting for my moment,
Preparing spiritually.
The journey is only meant for me,
These camels of conservativity
Carrying years of untapped creativity
Devoting time indefinitely
And connecting to her cosmically
Fulfilling the dreams I see.

Awake

The life embracing me,
Constantly, in duality.
Know the future, I will see,
The path that is left for me,
Passing by cosmically,
As I project astrally
Perpetually into being me.

Serene

It's tranquility,
Scenery warm, emotion blue.
Dreams coming true.

Memory

Bare feet padding through,
Lost in forever with you.
Cherished memory.

Beach

Let's go back to the beach,
When it was just you and me.
Dreaming of distant tomorrows,
Existing void of sorrows.

Let's go back to the beach,
Play in the arcade indefinitely,
Chasing the waves, finding shells,
Forgetting everyone but ourselves.

Let's go back to the beach,
Together as a family.
Create new memories,
Because we've achieved those dreams.

Lets go back to the beach,
When life's too loud to think.
Find strength with the memory,
Family is the best scenery.

Writing

The scratching of the pen against the paper,
The slide of my arm running across the desk.
The small movements of my hand to operate the utensil,
The survival of completing a test.
The shock of getting lost in your work,
The strong emotions expressed with time.
The surprise of aching muscles from writing too much,
The satisfaction of completing a novel or even a line.
The state of writing is something amazing,
The secret is to write what you feel;
The strategy is easy to follow and believe
The story will come and go but will always fulfill.

www.ingramcontent.com/pod-product-compliance
Lightning Source LLC
Chambersburg PA
CBHW051001030426
42339CB00007B/440